Frogs

Frogs

Edited by
Lynn Hughes

CONGDON & WEED
New York

What a wonderful bird the frog are –
When he stand he sit almost;
When he hop, he fly almost.
He ain't got no sense hardly;
He ain't got no tail hardly either.
When he sit, he sit on what he ain't got
almost.

THE MEXICAN FROG

Croak! said the Toad, I'm hungry, I think,
Today I've had nothing to eat or to drink.
I'll crawl to the garden and jump through
    the pales,
And there I'll dine nicely on slugs and on
    snails;
Ho, ho! quoth the Frog, is that what you
    mean?
Then I'll hop away to the next meadow
    stream,
There I will drink and eat worms and slugs
    too
And then I shall have a good dinner like
    you.

NURSERY RHYME

Croak, said the Frog—
I'm hungry, I think;
To-day I've had nothing
To eat or to drink.

The Frog says Aristotle liveth quietly all the time of cold weather and never stirreth abroad, until time of coite or conjunction. And then by croaking voice he allureth the Female and stirreth her to Venevie. These are Frogs called Seafrogs, of whom Tullie speaketh after this sort. They overcover themselves with sand, a knack used of them to beguile little fishes, and as they come by them, they step out and catch them and so swallow them up.

JOHN MAPLET
A GREEN FOREST

At Woodlawn I heard the dead cry;
I was lulled by the slamming of iron,
A slow drip over stones,
Toads brooding in wells.
All the leaves stuck out their tongues;
I shook the softening chalk of my bones,
Saying,
Snail, snail, glister me forward,
Bird, soft-sigh me home.
Worm, be with me
This is my hard time.

THEODORE ROETHKE
THE LOST SON

Be kind and tender to the Frog
   And do not call him names
As 'Shiny skin' or 'Polly wog'
   Or likewise Ugly James
Or Gape-a-grin or Toad gone wrong
   Or Billy Bandy Knees
The Frog is justly sensitive
   To epithets like these.
No animal will more repay
   A treatment kind and fair
At least so lonely people say
   Who keep a frog (and by the way,
They are extremely rare).

HILAIRE BELLOC
THE FROG

Also the Lord said unto Moses, say thou unto Aaron stretch thou out thy hand with thy rod upon the streams, upon the rivers and upon the ponds and cause Frogs to come upon the land of Egypt. And the Frogs came up and covered the land of Egypt. And the sorcerers did likewise with their sorceries and brought Frogs upon the land of Egypt. Then Pharaoh called for Moses and Aaron and said Pray unto the Lord that he may take away the Frogs from me, and from my people, and I will let the people go that they may do sacrifice unto the Lord. And Moses said unto Pharaoh, concerning me, command when I shall pray for thee and thy servants and thy people to destroy the Frogs from thee, and from thy houses that they may remain in the River only. Then Moses and Aaron went out from Pharaoh and Moses cried unto the Lord concerning the Frogs which he had sent unto Pharaoh. And the Lord did according to the saying of Moses, so the Frogs died in the Houses and in the Townes and in the fields. And they gathered them together in heaps, and the land stank of them.

HOLY BIBLE
EXODUS 8 v–xiv

With their lithe strong legs
Some frogs are able
To thump upon double-
Bass strings though pond water deadens
   and clogs.
But you, bullfrog, you pump out
Whole fogs full of horn – a threat
As of a liner looming. True
That, first hearing you
Disgorging your gouts of darkness like a
   wounded god,
Not utterly fantastical I expected
(As in some antique tale depicted)
A broken-down bull up to its belly in mud.
Sucking black swamp up, belching out
   black cloud
And a squall of gudgeon and lilies.

                    A surprise

To see you, a boy's prize,
No bigger than a rat – all dumb silence
In your little old woman hands.

TED HUGHES
BULL FROG

He was a frog and she was a frog,
And they built a house in a hollow log.
He was a fine big handsome fellow;
She was a beauty green and yellow.
He said that she was a wife most rare;
She said that he was beyond compare.
While as for their home in the hollow log,
It was just a palace, declared each frog.
And as for their baby why he
Was just a marvellous prodigy.
If he did but open his mouth and croak,
They laughed and thought it a splendid
    joke.
I tell you this story that you may see
How happy a frog and his wife may be.

WHEN ALL IS YOUNG

Nevertheless, a frog was found, within my time, in the grassy meadows near Waterford, and brought to court alive before Robert Poer and many others, both English and Irish. And when they had beheld it with great astonishment, at last Duvenold, King of Ossory, a man of sense among his people, and faithful, beating his head, and having deep grief at heart, spoke thus. 'That reptile is the bearer of doleful news to Ireland.' And uttering a sort of prognostic, he said, that it portended, without doubt, the coming of the English, their threatened conquest, and the subjugation of his own nation. No man, however, will venture to suppose that this reptile was ever born in Ireland; for the mud there does not, as in other countries, contain the germs from which green frogs are bred. It may have happened that some particle of the germ had been exhaled into the clouds by the heat of the atmosphere, and wafted hither by the force of the winds; but the better opinion is, that the frog was brought over by accident in a ship from some neighbouring port, and being cast on shore, succeeded in subsisting and maintaining life for a time, as it is not a venomous animal.

GIRALDUS CAMBRENSIS
THE TOPOGRAPHY OF IRELAND

And while Mr Jeremy sat disconsolately on the edge of his boat – sucking his sore fingers and peering down into the water – a much worse thing happened; a really frightful thing it would have been, if Mr Jeremy had not been wearing a macintosh!

BEATRIX POTTER
THE TALE OF MR JEREMY FISHER

But the land Frogs are ingendered out of Egs of whom we discourse at this present; and therefore they both suffer copulation, lay their Egges and bring forth young ones on the land. When the Egge breaketh or is hatched there cometh forth a little black thing like a piece of flesh, having no part of a living creature upon them, besides their eyes and their tails, and within short space after their feet are formed; and their tail divided into two parts, which tail becometh their hinder-legs. The heads of these young *Gyrini* which we call in English Horsenails; because they resemble a Horse-nail in their similitude, whose head is great, and the other part small, for with his tail he swimmeth.

EDWARD TOPSELL
HISTORY OF SERPENTS

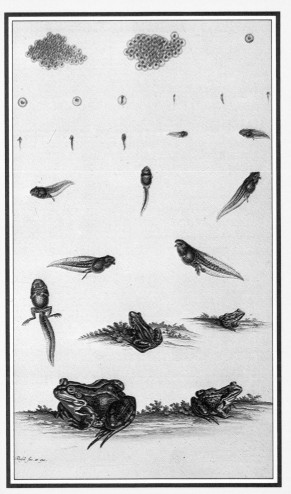

Frogs sit more solid
than anything sits. In mid-leap they are
parachutists falling
in a free fall. They die on roads
with arms across their chests and
heads high.
I love frogs that sit
like Buddha, that fall without
parachutes, that die
like Italian tenors.
Above all, I love them because,
pursued in water, they never
panic so much that they fail
to make stylish triangles
with their ballet dancer's legs.

NORMAN MACCAIG
FROGS

It has been often asserted that young frogs and fish will fall from the clouds in storms and it has often (been) wrongly asserted when the phenomena has sprung from natural causes – I have seen thousands of young frogs crossing a common after a shower but I found that they had left their hiding places and pursued their journeys after the shower began early in the morning early risers may see swarms of young frogs leaving their birthplaces and emigrating as fast as they can hop to new colonys and as soon as the sun gets strong they hide in the grass as well as they are abel to await the approach of night to be able to start again but if in the course of the day showers happen to fall they instantly seize the chance and proceed on their journey till the sun looks out and puts a stop to their travelling as to young fish I always found them in holes that were near neighbours to brooks.

JOHN CLARE
LETTERS

Toad sat straight down in the middle of the dusty road, his legs stretched out before him, and stared fixedly in the direction of the disappearing motor-car. He breathed short, his face wore a placid, satisfied expression, and at intervals he faintly murmured, 'Poop-poop!' The Mole was busy trying to quiet the horse, then he went to look at the cart. It was indeed a sorry sight. Panels and windows smashed, axles hopelessly bent, one wheel off, sardine tins scattered and the bird in the bird-cage sobbing pitifully and calling to be let out. The Toad never answered a word, or budged from his seat in the road; so they went to see what was the matter with him. They found him in a sort of trance, a happy smile on his face, his eyes fixed on the dusty wake of their destroyer. At intervals he was still heard to murmur, 'Poop-poop!' The rat shook him by the shoulder 'Are you coming to help us, Toad?' he demanded sternly. 'Glorious, stirring sight!' murmured Toad, never offering to move. 'The poetry of motion!' 'The *real* way to travel! The only way to travel! Here today – in next week tomorrow! Villages skipped, towns and cities jumped – always somebody else's horizon! O bliss! O poop-poop! Oh my! O my!'

KENNETH GRAHAME
THE WIND IN THE WILLOWS

I'm a Nobody! who are you?
Are you – Nobody – too?
Then there's a pair of us!
Don't tell! they'd advertise – you know!

How dreary – to be – somebody!
How public – like a Frog –
To tell one's name – the livelong June –
To an admiring Bog!

EMILY DICKINSON

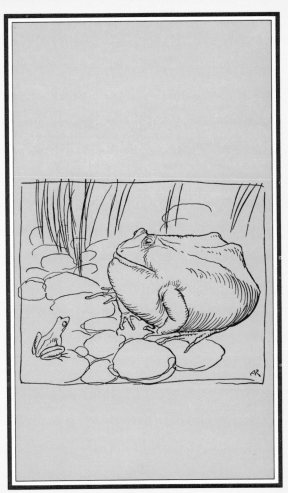

If a man take the tongue of a water frog and lay it upon the head of one that is asleep he shall speak in his sleep and reveal the secrets of his heart: but if he will know the secrets of a woman he must cut it out of the Frog alive, and turn the Frog away again, making certain characters upon the Frog's tongue, and so lay the same upon the panting woman's heart, and let him ask her what questions he will, and she shall answer to him all the truth and reveal all the secret faults that ever she hath committed. Now, if this magical foolery were true, we had more need of Frogs than of Justices of the Peace, or Magistrates in the Common-wealth.

Some again do write, that if a woman take a Frog and spit three times in her mouth she shall not conceive with child that year. Also if Dogs eat the pottage wherein a Frog hath been, it maketh him dumb and cannot bark. These and such like vanities have the ancient Heathens (ignorant of God) firmly believed.

EDWARD TOPSELL
HISTORY OF SERPENTS

Tab III

A.I.Rösel fecit et exc.

Every spring in temperate zones, and at the start of the rainy season in tropical regions, the male toads sing some of the world's loveliest love songs. To pay no attention to them, or to mistake them for something else, is to deny yourself a great pleasure. In my own neighbourhood not far from New York City the toad concerts usually begin in late March. They are preceded a week or two earlier by a sort of warming up performance given by tiny tree frogs called spring peepers, which have high sweet trilling voices, and by decidedly unmusical leopard frogs and wood-frogs, which sound like a distant procession of ox-drawn wagons, the axles of which badly need lubrication. Then the toads strike up. To produce their calls they first inflate a balloon-like pouch at their throats. Then, keeping their mouths tightly closed, they drive air back and forth between lungs and mouth across their vocal cords. The inflated pouch works as a resonator and works so well it causes the whole animal to vibrate. The calls are melodious trills of medium pitch often audible a quarter of a mile or more away. The toads do most of their calling after dark and usually do not begin until the temperature is steady at about sixty degrees. A rise to seventy brings out the whole glorious chorus.

ROBERT FROMAN
SPIDERS, SNAKES AND OTHER OUTCASTS

Tab XVI

Roesel a R. fecit et exc.

All year the flax-dam festered in the heart
Of the townland; green and heavy headed
Flax had rotted there, weighted down by
    huge sods.
Daily it sweltered in the punishing sun.
Bubbles gargled delicately, bluebottles
Wove a strong gauze of sound around the smell.
There were dragon-flies, spotted butterflies,
But best of all was the warm thick slobber
Of frogspawn that grew like clotted water
In the shade of the banks.

    Then one hot day when fields were rank
With cowdung in the grass the angry frogs
Invaded the flax-dam; I ducked through hedges
To a coarse croaking that I had not heard
Before. The air was thick with a bass chorus.
Right down the dam gross-bellied frogs were
    cocked
On sods; their loose necks pulsed like sails.
    Some hopped:
The slap and plop were obscene threats.
    Some sat
Poised like mud grenades, their blunt heads
    farting.
I sickened, turned, and ran. The great slime
    kings
Were gathered there for vengeance and I knew
That if I dipped my hand the spawn would
    clutch it.

SEAMUS HEANEY
DEATH OF A NATURALIST

There is, to this day, a marble chimney-piece at Charsworth, with the print of a toad upon it and a tradition of the manner in which it was found. In the Memoirs of the Academy of Sciences there is an account of a toad found alive and healthy in the heart of a very thick elm, without the smallest entrance or egress. In the year 1731 there was another found near Nantes in the heart of an old oak without the smallest issue to its cell and the discoverer was of the opinion, from the size of the tree, that the animal could not have been confined there less than eighty or a hundred years without sustenance and without air.

OLIVER GOLDSMITH
HISTORY OF ANIMATED NATURE

Lebault advises that if your ponds be not very large and roomy that you often feed your fish. He says that frogs and ducks do much harm but allows that water frogs be good meat especially in some months if they be fat: but you are to note that he is a Frenchman; and we English hardly believe him. A gentleman of tried honesty told me he saw in a hot summer day a large carp swim near to the top of the water with a Frog upon his head, and that he upon that occasion caused his pond to be let dry: and I say, of seventy or eighty carps, only found five or six in the said pond, and those very sick and lean, and with every one a Frog sticking so fast upon the head of the said carps that the Frog would not be got off without extreme force or killing and the gentleman that did affirm this to me, told me he saw it, and did declare his belief to be (and I also believe the same) that he thought the other carps that were so strangely lost, were so killed by Frogs, and then devoured.

IZAAK WALTON
THE COMPLEAT ANGLER

Mr Froggie went a-courtin' an' he did ride;
Sword and pistol by his side.

He went to Missus Mousie's hall,
Gave a loud knock and gave a loud call.

'Pray, Missus Mousie, air you within?'
'Yes, kind sir, I set an' spin.'

He tuk Miss Mousie on his knee,
An' sez, 'Miss Mousie, will ya marry me?'

Miss Mousie blushed an' hung her head,
'You'll have t'ask Uncle Rat,' she said.

'Not without Uncle Rat's consent
Would I marry the Pres-i-dent.'

Uncle Rat jumped up an' shuck his fat side,
To think his niece would be Bill Frog's bride.

Nex' day Uncle Rat went to town,
To git his niece a weddin' gown.

Whar shall the weddin' supper be?
'Way down yander in a holler tree.

First come in was a Bumble-bee,
Who danced a jig with Captain Flea.

Next come in was a Butterfly,
Sellin' butter very high.

An' when they all set down to sup,
A big gray goose come an' gobbled 'em all up.

An' this is the end of one, two, three,
The Rat an' the Mouse an' the little Froggie.

FROG WENT A-COURTIN'

Can these, indeed, be voices that so greet
   The twilight still? I seem to hear
Oboe and symbal in a rhythmic beat
With bass-drum and bassoon; their drear
And droll crescendo louder growing,
Then falling back, like waters ebbing,
   flowing, –
Back to silence sweet.

FLORENCE EARLE COATES
THE FROGS

βρεκεκεκὲξ κοὰξ κοάξ
Brekekekex, ko-ax, ko-ax,
Children of fountain and lake
    Let us awake
Our full choir shout, as flutes cry out,
    In symphony of clear-voiced song.
Those songs we loved in the Marshland
    above,
Which the revel-tipsy throng all crapulous
    and gay
At our doorsteps regaled us on the holy
    Pitcher day.
Loud and louder our chant must flow
Sing if ye ever sang of yore,
When in sunny and glorious days
Through the rushes and march-flags
    springing
On we swept, in the joy of singing
Myriad – diving roundelays
Or when fleeing the storm we went
Down to the depths, and our choral song
Wildly raised to a loud and long
Bubble-bursting accompaniment
Stretching all our throats with song
Shouting, crying all day long.
Brekekekex, ko-ax, ko-ax,
Brekekekex, ko-ax, ko-ax.
βρεκεκεκὲξ κοὰξ κοάξ.

ARISTOPHANES
FROGS

Kexy, Friend of Fairies.

The following is useful when proud flesh forms in a wound, namely, white alum reduced to powder the same powder being applied thereon. Another for the same purpose. Take a toad that can scarcely creep, beat it with a rod, till irritated, it swells and dies. Then put it in an earthen pot, closing the same so that no smoke can come out or air enter in. Then burn it till it is reduced to ashes, and apply the same to the part.

THE PHYSICIANS OF MYDDFAI

The toad beneath the harrow knows
Exactly where each tooth point goes;
The butterfly upon the road
Preaches contentment to that toad.

RUDYARD KIPLING
PAGET M P

Illustration acknowledgements

5 Valerie Ganz from a photograph by Ardea Wildlife in Colour

7 Hon. Eleanor Vere Boyle: 'Croak said the Frog', *Mary Evans Picture Library*

9 'The Morning Walk' exhibited at the Crystal Palace, 1851. *Mary Evans Picture Library*

11 Arthur Rackham: The Frogs and the Well. *Mary Evans Picture Library*

13 'BTB' from Hilaire Belloc: The Book of Beasts. *Gerald Duckworth Ltd*

15 Maria Sybillia Merian: Frog and Two Snakes' Heads (detail). *Royal Library Windsor*

17 G. Mützel: Bull Frogs, engraved by H. & J. von Jahrmargh from A. E. Brehm. *Merveilles de la Nature*

19 Rosel von Rosenhof: Green Frogs from Ranarum. *British Museum (Natural History)*

21 The Variable Green Toad. *British Museum (The Mansell Collection)*

23 Beatrix Potter: The Tale of Mr Jeremy Fisher. *Copyright under the Berne Convention Frederick Warne Ltd*

25 Rosel von Rosenhof: Green Frog's Spawn, Tadpoles and Juvenile Frogs, Ranarum. *British Museum (Natural History)*

27 J. de Gheyn: Frogs. Pen and ink. *National Gallery of Scotland*

The author and the publisher gratefully acknowledge permission to use material in copyright from the following:

Gerald Duckworth & Co. Ltd for Hilaire Belloc's 'The Frog'; Doubleday & Co. for Theodore Roethke's 'The Lost Son'; Messrs Faber & Faber for Ted Hughes's 'Bull Frog'; Eyre Methuen Ltd for Kenneth Grahame's *The Wind in the Willows*; Chatto & Windus Ltd for Norman MacCaig's 'Frogs'; Frederick Warne & Co. for Beatrix Potter's *The Tale of Mr Jeremy Fisher*; The National Trust of Great Britain for Rudyard Kipling's 'Paget MP'; G. Bell & Co. for 'Spiders, Snakes and other Outcasts' by Robert Froman; Seamus Heaney and Messrs Faber & Faber for 'Death of a Naturalist'.

Thanks are also due to Mrs V. Williams at the Westminster City Library, to the staff at HM Library, Windsor Castle, to the staff at the Prints and Drawings Room at the British Museum, to Mrs Ross at the National Museum of Scotland, to Valerie Ganz, Blanche Davies and Jane Gelfman, for their help.